Horizontal Verticals:

These involve the expansion of a company's offerings across different industries.

For example, a company manufacturing software for the healthcare sector may diversify into providing similar solutions for the finance industry.

Vertical Integration:

This involves the expansion of a company's operations within the same industry but across different stages of the value chain.

For instance, a car manufacturer might integrate vertically by starting to produce its own steel or opening retail outlets.

In the dynamic landscape of the business world, companies constantly seek ways to diversify and expand their operations. One strategic approach to achieve this is by adopting business verticals.

A business vertical, also known as industry vertical, refers to a specialized segment within a broader market or industry.

This book delves into the significance of business verticals, why they are essential for organizational growth, and how companies can effectively establish and manage them.

Understanding Business Verticals

Business verticals are essentially specialized business units or segments that focus on a specific product or service within a broader market.

They can be categorized into three main types:

Specialized Verticals:

 Companies may also create specialized business units to focus on a niche market or a particular customer segment.

 This could include targeting a specific demographic, such as luxury products for high-income consumers.

Importance of Business Verticals

Diversification and Risk Mitigation:

Business verticals allow companies to diversify their product or service offerings, reducing dependence on a single market.

This diversification acts as a risk mitigation strategy, as economic fluctuations or challenges in one industry may be balanced by success in another.

Market Penetration:

 Companies can use business verticals to penetrate new markets or demographics.

 By tailoring products or services to the unique needs of a specific segment, they increase their chances of success in those markets.

Competitive Advantage:

 Establishing business verticals can provide a competitive edge by allowing a company to differentiate itself from competitors.

 Specialization often leads to a better understanding of customer needs and more tailored solutions.

Economies of Scale:

 Through vertical integration, companies can achieve economies of scale by controlling more stages of the production or distribution process.

 This can result in cost savings and increased efficiency.

Adaptability to Market Trends:

The business environment is subject to rapid changes and evolving trends.

Business verticals provide companies with the agility to adapt quickly to emerging market trends and capitalize on new opportunities.

Strategies for Establishing Business Verticals

Market Research and Analysis:

Before diving into creating business verticals, comprehensive market research is crucial.

This involves identifying potential segments, understanding customer needs, and evaluating the competition.

Strategic Planning:

 Develop a clear and comprehensive strategic plan that outlines the objectives, target markets, and key performance indicators for each business vertical.

 This plan should align with the overall corporate strategy.

Resource Allocation:

 Allocate resources effectively, ensuring that each business vertical receives the necessary financial, human, and technological resources.

 This involves balancing investment and risk across the different segments.

Talent Acquisition and Development:

 Building a capable team for each business vertical is essential.

 Recruit individuals with expertise in the specific industry and provide ongoing training to keep them updated on industry trends.

Technological Integration:

Leverage technology to streamline operations and enhance efficiency across business verticals.

This may involve implementing advanced software, automation, or data analytics tools.

Customer-Centric Approach:

 Tailor products and services to meet the unique needs of each target market.

 A customer-centric approach ensures that the offerings resonate with the specific preferences and expectations of the intended audience.

Collaboration and Synergy:

 Encourage collaboration and synergy among different business verticals within the organization.

 This can foster innovation, cross-selling opportunities, and the sharing of best practices.

Performance Monitoring and Adaptation:

Implement robust performance monitoring mechanisms to track the success of each business vertical.

Regularly review key performance indicators and adapt strategies based on market feedback and changing conditions.

Case Study: Amazon's Business Verticals

Amazon, a global e-commerce giant, provides a compelling case study on the effective implementation of business verticals.

The company began as an online bookstore but quickly expanded into diverse verticals, including:

Amazon Web Services (AWS):
 A cloud computing platform that caters to businesses' computing, storage, and database needs. This vertical has become a significant revenue generator for Amazon.

Amazon Prime Video:
 Venturing into the entertainment industry, Amazon created a streaming service to compete with established players like Netflix.

Amazon Fresh and Whole Foods: In the grocery sector, Amazon acquired Whole Foods and introduced Amazon Fresh, showcasing the company's foray into the food retail vertical.

Kindle and Alexa Devices: The hardware vertical includes the Kindle e-reader and Alexa-enabled devices, demonstrating Amazon's expansion into the electronics and technology market.

Through these strategic moves, Amazon diversified its revenue streams, reduced dependency on its e-commerce platform, and established a strong presence in various industries.

Challenges and Considerations

While business verticals offer numerous benefits, their establishment is not without challenges.

Companies must navigate potential pitfalls, such as:

Resource Constraints:

 Allocating resources across multiple verticals can strain a company's financial and human resources.

Coordination and Communication:

 Maintaining effective communication and coordination between different business verticals is crucial to avoid conflicts and ensure a cohesive organizational strategy.

Market Saturation:

In highly competitive markets, finding a niche for each business vertical becomes challenging, and saturation may occur.

Adaptability:

Companies must be agile and adaptable to changes in market conditions. Rigid structures or resistance to change can hinder the success of business verticals.

Business verticals are indispensable tools for companies aiming to thrive in today's ever-evolving business landscape.

Their strategic implementation allows for diversification, risk mitigation, and the ability to capitalize on emerging opportunities.

By carefully planning, allocating resources, and fostering a customer-centric approach, organizations can successfully establish and manage business verticals.

The case study of Amazon exemplifies how a company can leverage verticals to become a global leader across multiple industries.

While challenges exist, the rewards for effective implementation are substantial, making business verticals a key driver of organizational growth and sustainability.

Hopefully, the space we provided on each page will allow you to take notes and cater this information to your business...

www.ingramcontent.com/pod-product-compliance
Lightning Source LLC
Chambersburg PA
CBHW072332270726

48658CB00016B/2373